Copyrighted material

by Jordyn Wright

Copyrighted material

Copyright

Copyright © 2021 J. Brielle Handmade Goods

Published by Read Wright Publishing
P.O. Box 1764, Brazoria, TX 77422

The Clean Truth About Starting A Business for Teens

All rights reserved. No part of this publication may be reproduced, distributed, or transmitted in any form or by any means, including photocopying, recording, or other electronic or mechanical methods, without the prior written permission of the publisher, except in the case of brief quotations embodied in critical reviews and certain other noncommercial uses permitted by copyright law.

This is a nonfiction publication. No facts have been altered. The author and the publisher are not responsible for the results accrued from the advice in this book.

Read Wright Publishing

ISBN: 978-1-7374189-0-0

Table of Contents
Recipe for Mixing Up a Batch of Business

Preface — 11

Intro — 19

Step 1: The Prep

   First Ingredient: Motivated Mindset — 29

   Second Ingredient: Passion and purpose — 39

   Third Ingredient: inspiring your "why" — 49

Step 2: Measure

   Fourth Ingredient: Research and resources — 59

   Fifth Ingredient: Custom Customer — 69

   Sixth Ingredient: YOUniquely You — 77

Step 3: Mix and Pour

   Seventh Ingredient: Marketing Mix (The 4 Ps) — 87

   Eighth Ingredient: Budgeting Basics — 101

   Ninth Ingredient: Finding financing — 109

Table of Contents
Recipe for Mixing Up a Batch of Business

Outro — 118

Postface — 120

Glossary — 124

Resources — 127

Dedicated to my future...and yours.

IF YOU DON'T HAVE
BIG DREAMS OR
GOALS
YOU WILL END UP WORKING FOR
SOMEONE THAT DOES

-- Unknown

PREFACE

Hello friend! You must be ready to, or are at least a little bit curious about, starting your own business. Well, you found the right book. However, I want to warn you. If you are not sure about becoming an ***entrepreneur***, be prepared to be persuaded!

What exactly is an entrepreneur anyway? An entrepreneur is anyone that provides a product or service that solves a problem and or meets the needs of everyday people like you and me. They then sell their product or service to earn income and build wealth for themselves.

Entrepreneurs don't work for someone else, except the customer. They are the boss of their own business and make all the decisions. They take on the risk if the business fails and receive the greatest reward when it succeeds. It really is that simple...or is it?

The idea of not wanting to work for anyone else was already on my mind way back when I was in fourth grade. My mom had been telling me about how she worked in Human Resources. She said it was so stressful and she had to work in a tiny office all day. She also said she couldn't leave when she wanted, or ask for more pay, even when she was doing twice the amount of work she was supposed to.

These were the things that bothered me most. I know that not all jobs are like this, but at the time, this is what I believed. I vowed that unless I had to, I would never work for anyone else other than myself.

Later, when I was in sixth grade, I started J. Brielle Handmade Goods. At the time, I only made handmade soap. I chose to make soap because I had eczema when I was little. I could never get the soaps I liked. I always had to buy scentless white soaps because the chemicals from fragrances made me itch. Ugh! So, I found a solution to my soap problem and started a business that allowed me to have the kinds of bath products I wanted, make money, and be creative (something I LOVE to do) all at the same time!

At this point, I understood that not all jobs required you to stay inside of a tiny cubicle for fifteen hours. Yet, to this day, I still haven't heard one person in my family say they feel overpaid and underworked. So, I remain unswayed.

I wanted to work for no one but myself...and God. I decided that by starting my business early I could earn money my way, working for myself and toward my dreams. And after watching many episodes of Shark Tank, tons of YouTube videos, and even taking a few business classes, I realize that the idea of a teen running a real business is not unheard of or impossible.

Have you ever thought about making your own money and the different ways you could earn it? Whether it's baking, babysitting, or mowing lawns, making money as a teen is pretty common. Yet, the way our parents made money when they were our age doesn't have to be the same way we earn it.

I have another question for you. Have you ever thought to yourself, "I don't want to work for someone else when I grow up?" I have. While working for someone else isn't bad, it's not my idea of freedom. I want the ability to work in and of my own accord. I do not want to work on someone else's schedule or have them determine how much I get paid.

If this is how you feel too, pay close attention. If not, that's okay. Still follow along because what I am going to share with you is important either way.

Whatever your goal is for your future, start thinking about what you want your life to look like now! What is it that you love to do? How can you turn this into a business or career where you can earn money while having fun doing what you enjoy most?

The icing on the cake is that apart from running your own business, you will be helping others. All successful businesses will have employees someday. Your business will provide job opportunities for those that need it, as well as inspiration for those that also want to become entrepreneurs.

Now, before you say that you are ready to jump in, you need to know that the journey to owning your own business is super exciting, but not without challenges. It takes a lot of discipline and self-control. You must learn how to choose your priorities and manage your time well. This can sometimes mean not hanging out with your friends or working when you usually want to chill. You cannot be lazy! Your business must be one of your top priorities.

It requires your commitment, hard work, and a fearless spirit. Sometimes you may want to give up, or you may have someone try to discourage you. Some days you will make money and some days you won't. But trust me, in the end, it is so worth it! I want to give you a real look into what owning a business is like and how you can get started. So, if you are still reading this book, that must mean you are ready! Ok then, let's go!

NEVER BE LIMITED
BY OTHERS LIMITED IMAGINATIONS

-- Mae Jemison
Astronaut and First Black Woman to Travel into Space

INTRO

When I was little, I knew I wanted to change the world and already had some big ideas. Whenever someone asked me what I wanted to be when I grew up, I would say, "I want to be queen!" I wanted to be the leader of my own world. I also wanted to be a singer, artist, gymnast, and dancer all at the same time. Why not? There wasn't a law that said I couldn't. Whatever I was going to be, it would allow me to make up my own rules and follow my dreams.

Fast forward to when I was nine years old. I would sneak into my bathroom to make homemade slimes and secret concoctions of soaps, shampoos, and other things from the supplies I found in my mom's closet. She would get so mad when she found out I had used all of her hair products and expensive body washes to make my own. I loved the way they smelled, but because I had eczema, it would irritate my skin terribly. She eventually saw my frustration and felt a little sorry for me (although, I think she was still mad that I used all of her stuff). So, she took me shopping to find some soaps that I would like and wouldn't negatively affect my skin.

I have always loved going into the beauty and bath stores inside of the mall where my mom would buy her favorite products. All the colors, different shapes, and the way they smelled made me want them even more. My mom did let me try a few of them, but then complain that they cost way too much to buy so often.

Eventually, we started searching for ways to make scented and colorful soaps at home. This was really fun! I watched so many YouTube videos of soapmaking, and once I got the hang of it, I ended up making a ton of them.

My dad told me I should try to sell my soaps because I had made so many. At first, I was afraid to ask someone to buy them. I just sort of gave them away if people in my family wanted one. Then my mom encouraged me to take a tray of soaps to my neighbor and ask them if they wanted to buy one. They bought five! That was great and all, but I still wasn't sure about selling my soaps.

I'm just a kid. How could I compete with bigger companies and others who have been in the soap game longer than me? After a lot of persuading from my mom, I started selling them at my church. I did get several sales, but I just thought they wanted to support me because I was a kid, not because they took my business seriously.

Then one day, a girl I knew who had eczema too, tried my soap. When she and her mom told me how much they liked it and wanted more, I knew I was on to something! After that, I wanted to build a soap business that would help kids like me love to take baths. I wanted to have my own store where I could have an assembly line to show my customers how my products are made. I wanted my soaps to be on the shelves of Walmart, Target, and other places. Here I was, only 10 years old. Could I have my own business even though I was so young?

My mom always told me there is nothing impossible for me, that there are no limits. The only limit to my dreams would be what I decided they would be. So, I did decide. I decided that I would be limitless. You can be limitless too! And if no one has told you yet, you are *already* limitless. You have untapped potential that is begging to exploit itself. It just needs you to see it and give it the opportunity.

That is why I wrote this book especially for you. Yes...you! To help you create your own business and tap into that entrepreneurial spirit that lives inside of you. I bet you didn't even know it was there! You were thinking, "My greatest accomplishment has been getting my homework turned in on time," weren't you? I challenge you to think a little bigger. I tapped into my imagination and the potential I have to do anything I set my mind to. Now it's your turn and you are exactly the right person to do it.

Why? Well, did you know that you and I are among some of the most influential people in the world? GEN-Z (that's us) is the most creative and innovative generation to grace the planet, IMHO. Almost everybody is watching our generation. They want to see what fashion ideas, new tech, dances, or social platforms we will create. You and I have a major impact on the world already and we are still teenagers. That is powerful!

So, you've heard my story and I have given you plenty of reasons why you should at least think about starting your own business. Now it's time for me to truly convince you. Enough of the pep talk. You are definitely ready to get this entrepreneurial party started.

Remember I told you early on, once you start reading, there's no turning back. You're in this with me and together we are going to take the first steps into building your business. After you read this book, you will have only one of two choices to make. Either get started with living your dreams or keep your dreams in your head. Which will you choose?

The Clean Truth About STARTING A BUSINESS for Teens

STEP ONE: THE PREP

Motivated Mindset

Passion and Purpose

Inspiring your "why"

The first thing I do before I create any of my products is make sure I have everything I need. This includes having the right perspective.

YOU CAN'T TALK LIKE A
FAILURE AND EXPECT TO BE

SUCCESSFUL

-- Germany Kent
Author, Journalist, Social Media Expert

First Ingredient
Motivated Mindset

Starting a business can be very scary. Especially when you are trying to figure things out by yourself. I mean, think about it. We are already trying to navigate our crazy teenage world and all of its demands! How do we get in the headspace of becoming a business owner and take on even more responsibility?

When I first started, I wasn't very confident in my products, let alone myself. I used to be so negative. When people first told me that my products were good enough to sell, I downplayed their compliments and made excuses about why I wasn't ready to go all official with my business.

Although I did like what I made, they were made by *me*. And who am I in comparison to big companies or other small businesses that have been selling soaps for years?

I eventually decided to begin selling my products, but my lack of confidence affected me and my ability to interact with potential customers. Everyone had to tell me to speak louder and look each person in the eyes.

All I heard was that I was weak and an overall disappointment. I felt I could never get over my fears, never be loud enough, strong enough, or confident enough. It took a toll on me and eventually I decided to quit.

I lost a lot of customers and let quite a few people down. Most importantly, I let myself down. When I realized this, something struck me. I understood that owning a business wasn't just about me. It was about pushing past my fears and not allowing them to cripple me. It was about serving others and seeing the smiles on their faces when they got their products. It also meant setting an example for my brothers and being a leader in my community.

My business starts with me but doesn't end there. It is a seed, and if other people saw it growing, then maybe they would feel inspired to start one too. I had to change my **mindset** from negative to positive. I had to remember my inspiration so that I could stay motivated.

If you don't have the right mindset when starting your business, you will give up easily too, forget your faith, and lose confidence quickly. I'm not going to lie. I can still get down sometimes because owning a business is a lot! The thing is, that's okay as long as I don't give up. I love what I do, and people need to see that. I may not be on the global stage just yet, but I am creating small ripple effects that will eventually cause tsunamis across the entire world!

The same goes for you. You don't have to have a perfect product, the most confidence, or 100 thousand followers. You still have influence. The smallest disturbance inside of a closed system can change it completely. You can be that disturbance to disrupt the status quo. All you have to do is believe that you can and keep a positive mindset.

Not to sound like your parents or anything, but your thoughts can be the difference between success and complete destruction. A negative mindset seriously affects your performance. If you are thinking negatively, your mind shuts down, and you cannot physically, mentally, or spiritually give 100% of yourself to anything.

If you want to be successful, then you are going to need to know how to stay positive without having ***toxic positivity*** (also known as suppressing true feelings of sadness and frustration), which can lead to spiritual and mental damage. There is a huge difference.

To do this, you need to first acknowledge your gifts, your feelings, and your flaws (which we all have by the way). Then, you need to accept them just the way they are because they make up the unique person that is you. I know this is easier said than done. Trust me, it makes things way better. Confidence in yourself doesn't mean you have reached perfection. It means that you love and accept the way God has made you. And we know everything God makes is good!

Also, as a business owner, you must be a leader, not a follower. This isn't to say you shouldn't be willing to listen to others who are more knowledgeable than you or take valuable advice when offered. You should always be teachable. However, being a follower will likely cause you to struggle in your own business if you are easily convinced to quit, change, or give up because of others around you. Or, you will want to do what everybody else does. Not good. We will talk more about this in a later chapter, but just know, you've got to be confident in yourself and your choices. And while you may not be 100% there yet (let me tell you...nobody is), you must be confident ENOUGH to believe in your dreams, your style, and your choices even when others don't.

Another thing to keep in mind is that while working for yourself is great, it can be mentally challenging because you have to be responsible with your time. If you decide to procrastinate or veg out in front of the TV when you have orders to fill, there is no one else to blame but yourself when you lose customers. My advice would be to keep a motivated mindset and manage your time wisely. Don't give in to lazy habits.

On the other hand, we know that we can be harder on ourselves than others. There is not a real proven method that keeps us from getting upset with ourselves. However, if you find yourself getting angry and having negative thoughts about how you and your business are doing, take a break. Sometimes you may need to get away from it all and take note of how you can do better. Then, jump back in the game and keep it moving. Even billionaire CEOs make mistakes! It's part of the journey.

Susan Gale, a famous artist, once said, *"Don't be too hard on yourself, there are plenty of people willing to do that for you. Love yourself and be proud of everything you do. Even mistakes mean you are trying."*

I love this quote because I am very hard on myself. I have to remember to give myself grace.

As Ms. Gale said, plenty of people are more than happy to point out my flaws. Some may even tell me I will never be successful or criticize me and my business. I can't let this affect me. I must remember that I have to accept it when I mess up, fix the problem, and move on.

So, to wrap up the first ingredient, be grateful for the things you are good at and your daily wins, no matter how small. Stay confident and motivated each day. Putting these things into practice and making a good effort toward improving is part of having the right mindset for building a successful business.

TIPS FOR YOUR FIRST INGREDIENT

Tip #1: Acknowledge your gifts, your feelings, and your flaws. Then accept them just the way they are. They are what make you special.

Tip #2: Always be confident enough to believe in yourself, but teachable enough to leave room for growth.

Tip #3: When you get frustrated with your business, take a break, give yourself grace, and make note of what you can do better. then get back to work.

Complete the *Motivated Mindset* worksheet by scanning the QR Code found at the back of this book in the resource section.

PASSION IS
ENERGY

FEEL THE POWER THAT COMES FROM
FOCUSING ON WHAT EXCITES YOU

-- Oprah Winfrey
Actor, Author, Philanthropist, Producer

Second Ingredient
Passion and Purpose

I think my parents and friends would say that I have a lot of hobbies. However, I call them passions. I love learning about dogs, creating unique pieces of art, reading the Bible, and of course, researching solutions for healthy skin. I also love supporting entrepreneurship initiatives, especially among our generation.

Entrepreneurship is more than just finding a way to make money. It's about owning the way we do it. We are the future and we should not be bound by the limitations of previous generations. We should forge our own path. Are you with me?! (I imagine myself saying this in the middle of a huge GEN-Z convention wearing a fancy black suit…don't ask).

Back to the point, you've got to know what you are passionate about. Many times, our passions are found within our hobbies. When we are passionate about something, it leads us to our purpose. Why else would we have it?

What is **passion** anyway? It may not be what you think so let's be sure we have a clear definition. The dictionary's definition of passion is to have an uncontrollable emotion; an intense desire for enthusiasm.

I guess this is true. And while I don't disagree with this definition, I would add that passion is something that keeps you going. Whether you are feeling lazy, sad, tired, or anxious, you are driven to keep moving forward because you love what you are doing. Enthusiasm seems temporary, while passion on the other hand is long-term.

When I'm doing something I have a passion for, I feel almost like I'm living in a world of euphoria. Not in a way where someone might think I've lost it...well, maybe. What I mean is that when I do what I am passionate about, I don't think about my problems. I don't worry about if what I am doing is the right way, or if I'm doing it wrong. I know I will learn as I go along. I just want to focus on the enjoyment of completing the task.

My passion for my business gives me purpose. That purpose is to create natural bath and body products that make skincare routines fun and safe for teens with sensitive skin. Also, my business helps me to promote youth entrepreneurship, which is extremely important to me.

So, what are you passionate about? When you hear music, do you want to sing and dance all day? Do you feel compelled to write or draw all the time? If something stays on your mind, I mean you wake up thinking about it every day, that feeling is passion.

While you may not be passionate about the things I described, every one of us has been born with something that drives us. God gave us these intense feelings and talents so that we can use them to glorify Him while enjoying them ourselves. Whether it's a hobby, or you plan to become a professional at it, your passion can become your purpose. Your purpose can then become your business. They go hand in hand.

How do we find our passion? We may be born with them, but we still must develop them just like we do our brains.

Ask yourself if there is anything you love creating or a task you enjoy performing that you wouldn't mind doing for the rest of your life. Or, is there a topic you love reading about? Maybe there is a cause you are adamant about supporting?

If not, you can brainstorm with your friends and family. Ask them what you do most of your day that you seem to love. If you agree with them, great! You have found a passion. If not, do some research and explore products, services, and other ideas that interest you. By following these simple steps, you are sure to find a place to start.

Now, what do you do with this new knowledge? First things first. Look for ways to turn your passion into a business. Check out others who are doing what you want to do. See if people are interested in buying your product or service idea by reading customer reviews or social media responses from similar companies.

You might have a new and innovative idea that no one thought of before. That's great! The businesses you research don't have to be the exact thing you want to do, just something within the same field. For now, focus on getting a general sense of what your business idea looks like in the real world.

Next, you need to try it out. DO NOT invest too much money into this to start. Trust me, I did a lot of that at first. I wanted to get all kinds of soap molds, scents, colors, ingredients, and I didn't even know how to make soap yet. Now, half of the stuff I first bought I never even use.

So, start simple. Get the basic materials you will need to create a few samples or to perform the service you want a few times with family or friends. Once you have tried it out and done your initial research, you can start investing more time and money into your business.

This is where the fun begins. If you are not having fun, you might want to think about doing something else because you have to practice, practice, practice...even if you believe you are the best at doing what you do. There is always room for improvement, and you want to be sure that you are giving your clients the best product or service you can.

Then, find someone as passionate about what you want to do as you are. Don't be afraid to reach out to them and ask for advice. You will be surprised at how excited they will be to help.

When I started making lotions and body butter, I was horrible at it! Yes, there are a ton of videos on YouTube and an endless amount of books I could have read, but there is nothing better than learning directly from someone that loves making what you do...and is good at it.

I decided to reach out and ask someone if they would be willing to teach me and they said YES (thank you Ms. Chris and Ms. Susan)! After learning a basic recipe, I played with the formula and came up with my own. My customers love it!

There is someone in your family, at school, in your neighborhood, or community center that is waiting for you to ask. What's the worst that could happen? If they say no, you still have so many others that can help. Don't be afraid to ask for the help you need.

All these things go right along with having the right mindset because it is the basis of starting a successful business. Obstacles will frustrate you and you will make mistakes. Material prices may skyrocket, or your customers may flake on you. This is where passion kicks in. Passion encourages you to never give up and to find a way to do what you love to do.

🫧 TIPS FOR YOUR 🫧
SECOND INGREDIENT

Tip #1: Name one thing that you think about doing all the time. Think of ways you can turn it into a business.

Tip #2: Start with the basic materials and resources to practice your business idea before spending tons of money. Then build from there.

Tip #3: Practice, practice, practice and Have fun! If you're not having fun with your business, it's not worth doing.

Complete the *Passion and Purpose* worksheet by scanning the QR Code found at the back of this book in the resource section.

IF YOU REALLY CARE, YOU
DON'T HAVE TO BE PUSHED

THE VISION

PULLS YOU

-- Steve Jobs
CoFounder of Apple, Designer, Entrepreneur

Third Ingredient
INSPIRING YOUR "WHY"

Inspiration. Such a beautiful and sought-after thing. I don't believe there has ever been a day when I have not felt inspired by something or someone. Whether it was the due date of my homework, the urge to draw a picture, or the deep desire to get my own house because my brothers won't stay out of my room, inspiration comes to me in many forms.

Inspiration is different from passion in that passion flows from within, and inspiration comes from outside of us. Sometimes we get tired and our passion dims. However, the moment we see someone else doing what we love to do, or we are reminded of why we started our business, we are immediately inspired to get back in the game. We need both to keep us motivated toward our goals.

These together make up our WHY...why we want to be entrepreneurs in the first place and why succeeding matters.

It still amazes me how many times I hear another kid tell me that I have encouraged them in some way. Can you imagine? There have been times when someone I didn't know has come up to me and said, "Thank you Jordyn for motivating me to try making soaps," or start a new business, or talk to my child about entrepreneurship.

My business is more than just a way to make money. It's a way to serve, uplift, and inspire my community. All these things are my why. I know there are many, but my why is what keeps me from giving up on my dreams when things get hard.

Now, who or what inspires you, and what will be your why? Is it to be the youngest rocket builder in the world? Is it your hope to meet a certain financial goal in your life so that you can help out a parent or a cause?

Your "why" keeps you working toward your goal when you don't feel like doing anything at all, like vibing on the couch all day with your secret stash of candy while your parents are gone (not that I've ever done that). It helps you to avoid the distractions that may come.

Also, your "why" isn't just for you. It will flow *from* you as well. People in your family, community, and teens all over the world will be inspired to do something great because they saw you do it first! This is a responsibility you can't take too lightly. That is the power of being an ***influencer***. And trust me, our generation needs some good USEFUL influencing.

Let's not confuse inspiration with idolization. No hate to TikTok and Instagram, but you know sometimes we can get caught up looking at others and envying them because of what they have, are doing, or whom they know.

Sure, they may have great dance moves and a decent fashion sense, yet what makes them innovative or different? Nine times out of 10, looking for idols and not inspiration will lead you into depression, anxiety, and apathy. It's just so sad. The worst thing you can do is compare yourselves to others. There is no one like you and no one has your voice, your style, or your perspective. You are fearfully and wonderfully made. The world needs to hear from YOU!

Furthermore, having a business isn't just about making money. It allows you to give back to your community by doing philanthropy work. Talking to kids in schools, supporting a charity, and serving others is doing more than just giving. You are inspiring. Some little girl or boy, or even an adult will be encouraged by what you are doing. They will become the change *they* want to see in the world.

Working for yourself, building wealth for your family, and inspiring the next generation may all be a part of your why. These are the things that will keep you going, even when you get tired, frustrated, or scared.

If you try to do something challenging and you forget your "why" (or worse yet, don't have one), you will give up. So be sure to write them down in your journal, post them on your mirror, or make them your screensaver on your phone. Whatever you do, keep them in front of you all the time so that nothing will keep you from accomplishing your dreams!

TIPS FOR YOUR THIRD INGREDIENT

Tip #1: Write out your "why". What is your inspiration for starting your business and what keeps you motivated to push forward...even when things get hard.

Tip #2: Focus is important. Distractions will come, but you have to keep your eyes on the goal ahead of you.

Tip #3: Your "why" shouldn't *just* be about money. No amount of money will satisfy you. It should include a way of giving back to others.

Complete the *Inspiring Your "Why"* worksheet by scanning the QR Code found at the back of this book in the resource section.

The Clean Truth About STARTING A BUSINESS for Teens

STEP TWO: MEASURE

Research and resources

Custom Customer

YOUniquely You

Each time I make a soap bar, I take my time to measure out the right ingredients. It takes patience, but the right mix gives me the best results.

SUCCESS IS NOT TO BE MEASURED BY THE POSITION ONE HAS REACHED IN LIFE AS BY THE

OBSTACLES

WHICH "THEY" HAVE OVERCOME WHILE TRYING TO SUCCEED.

-- Booker T. Washington
Author, Educator, Presidential Advisor

Fourth Ingredient:
Research and Resources

When I first started soapmaking, I literally knew nothing about it. I did, however, know that it wasn't just throwing random ingredients together. So, what did I do? I researched. Initially, I went straight to YouTube University and watched a whole bunch of videos to learn more about my craft. I found several ways to easily make soap bars and was like, (★^O^★)! I was so excited that I started making soaps right away.

The first soaps I made turned out gloppy and uneven. I gave those to my brothers…LOL! The next ones I made looked great, but they burned because I added too much fragrance. My armpits have never been the same *tear*.

I had to learn about scent ratios and many other things before I could make them well. The moral of the story is that researching your craft is important...so that you don't burn your armpits. And, if you don't do enough research, you will waste so much time, let alone money!

How do you go about doing your research? Well, it's simple. The first thing you want to do is explore different sources to find information about your product or service. I use YouTube, Google, and books. Check out multiple resources instead of just a few. This helps to make sure you are not misinformed.

You might be overwhelmed during the research process because there will be a lot of information. So, I recommend taking notes. Use **shorthand** (abbreviations that you understand) to make notetaking easier.

Also, focus on one topic at a time. You can then take the information your resources have in common and merge them into one outline for that specific topic.

For example, if you are researching dog sitting, pick one topic about dog sitting to explore. It could be how much you should charge per hour. Look at different websites, articles, or call a dog sitting service and write down what you learn from each. Do they have consistent information? Then, it is probably a good place to start when setting your prices.

Staying organized while doing your research will help you to better understand the information you are gathering.

You can also get help from a mentor or expert through ***networking***. If you don't know anyone personally, find events that are specific to people like you. Reach out to a person of interest on Instagram or Facebook. Trust me. This helps. I have made so many connections that way.

It may be scary to talk to people you don't know at first, but most are nice and will be willing to help. Be sure to talk with your parents first before reaching out to someone. We don't want you talking with any creepers! Ugh!

Have one notebook or binder where you keep all of this information. It won't help if your notes are scattered everywhere. Or, if you have ripped out pieces of paper under your bed. Again, not that I have ever done that.

Most importantly, ask questions. Ask your parents, friends, teachers, or anyone who may be knowledgeable about your interests. Sometimes, we think things should be done one way when there really is a *better* way to do it. You would be surprised at how much information you can get from the people around you that will help your research process go smoother. If they don't know, they may be able to direct you to someone that does.

Research isn't always fun, but it is necessary. If you get bored, eat a snack, take a break, or listen to music while you are researching. These things help me when I find myself getting distracted or tired.

Don't spend so much time researching that you never get started. That would make this whole thing pointless. Don't overthink the process.

A LIST OF THINGS YOU NEED TO BE SURE TO RESEARCH INCLUDE:

- Who is selling a product or service like the one you are interested in providing?
- What do their customers say they like or dislike about it?

- How can you improve their product and make yours different?
- How do you make the product or provide the service?
- What resources do you need to get started?
- Who would want to buy the product?
- What laws or regulations do you have to follow?
- What costs, outside of making the product, do you need to think about?
- Will you enjoy making the product or providing the service as a business?

These are just some of the questions you might want to ask yourself. There are many more, but you will figure them out as you go.

Be sure that when you get started, you use all of the free **resources** you have available (ingredients, tools, mentors, etc.) before going out and buying more. Look around your home and see if you have materials you can use. Would someone in your family, a neighbor, teacher, or friend be willing to donate items you need? This will save you time, money, and frustration.

Sometimes you will have to find a way to get money for the things you need. We will talk about that in a later chapter. But for now, remember these few tips for your fourth ingredient in building a successful business.

TIPS FOR YOUR FOURTH INGREDIENT

Tip #1: Never start something you don't know anything about. If you do, it will be a waste of time, effort, and materials. Always do your research first.

Tip #2: Keep an open mind while learning. While you thought something should be done one way, you may find a better way of doing it.

Tip #3: Use as many free resources as you can to get started. Save your money for when you are ready to move forward with your business.

Complete the *Research and Resources* worksheet by scanning the QR Code found at the back of this book in the resource section.

**PEOPLE DON'T BY
PRODUCTS, THEY BUY**
SOLUTIONS

-- Meredith Hill
Global Travel Entrepreneur

Fifth Ingredient: Custom Customer

When you first start your business, you may try selling your product or service to everyone. Who wouldn't right? The more money the better. This is exactly what I did. My neighbors, people at church, my mom's friends, my family...I was trying to get everyone to buy my soaps. That's not exactly the best way to get customers.

Actually, I was missing out on reaching kids like me who really wanted my soaps and balms. I was losing a lot of customers by trying to sell to people who weren't interested in my products.

I'm not saying you shouldn't sell to those who want to buy, but try focusing on getting the attention of people that have the specific problem your product or service is solving.

As a business owner, you need to know who your customer is and how to serve them. Yes, you work for yourself now, however, part of owning a successful business is understanding exactly what your customer needs. This can be pretty difficult to do if you don't know anything about them.

This is why business owners create what is called an ***avatar***. An avatar is a very specific, fictional person you invent to represent your perfect customer.

You need to know everything about your avatar because they make up your ***target market***. Knowing who your target market is will help you get your product or service in front of the right people. They tell you which social media platforms to post on, what kinds of posts they like, competitors you should follow to find them, and so much more!

Things you need to know about your avatar include, where your avatar lives, what they do for fun, where they shop, their age, what type of friends they have, where they hang out, and their main problems.

No, this doesn't make you a stalker. Well, maybe, but not the creepy kind. Knowing so much about your avatar helps you to serve them better.

For example, one of my avatar's names is Ines. She is 14 years old, just starting the ninth grade, and lives in Terrell Hills, Texas. She is a gymnast and loves hanging out with her friends.

Ines does a lot of shopping online and on Instagram. She also loves going to different stores with her friends to check out the latest beauty brands and fashions for teens.

She earns a weekly allowance of $30 and uses her money to save up for things she wants to buy. Lately, she has been having a hard time with finding bath products that don't irritate her skin and it frustrates her.

Knowing what drives your avatar crazy is super important in helping you to communicate why they need you, and not someone else, to solve their problem.

Your avatar should be someone you can identify with so that you can better understand their needs. Spend time with people that match your avatar as often as you can. This will help you get to know them and discover their day-to-day problems.

Check out other companies your avatar might buy from. Follow them on social media and find out what you think is attracting people within your target market to their page. Use that knowledge to get your target market to come to you.

You should also know what their favorite payment options are. For example, a lot of people these days use Square, Venmo, and Cash App. Be prepared by having these downloaded on your phone or available on your website.

Here are more ways you can find insights about your target market:

- Survey your audience by asking them questions on social media.
- Go to competitor websites and social media pages to check out reviews and testimonials. See what they liked and didn't like about the products or services they reviewed.
- Simply ask your target market directly what they want to see in a product or service like

yours and what problems you can solve for them. This will make them feel super special.

- Try offering your product or service for a discount, or for free if you can, to someone who looks like your ideal customer. Always follow up to ask them what they thought.

TIPS FOR YOUR FIFTH INGREDIENT

Tip #1: Don't try to create a product to sell. Be a solution to your customer's problem.

Tip #2: Get to know your target audience well. Otherwise, you can't help them.

Tip #3: Know the benefits of your product or service so that you can explain why your Avatar needs it.

Complete the *Custom Customer* worksheet by scanning the QR Code found at the back of this book in the resource section.

IF YOU ARE ALWAYS TRYING TO BE
NORMAL, YOU WILL NEVER KNOW HOW

AMAZING

YOU CAN BE

-- Maya Angelou
Writer, Poet, Civil Rights Activist

Sixth Ingredient:
Youniquely You

I am weird. I'll just say it. I am really weird. I make weird faces and do weird dances. I use the word "THICC" to describe anything I like, or think is good. I still love singing all the *Hamilton* songs at the top of my lungs, even when everyone else in the house doesn't want to hear me sing. I've always loved being weird. Yet, when it came to my business, not so much.

I remember when I first started, I thought I should do what everybody else did in order to be successful. I tried to make all the products I saw other people make. I used the same scents they did and even tried to mimic their packaging. I thought that if I was like them more people would buy from me.

But the exact opposite was true. If I was like everybody else, I would just be another soap maker in a sea of soap makers. Most people would only buy from me because I just happened to be around, or they wanted to help me because I was a kidpreneur. They probably wouldn't buy again after the first time.

If I wanted more customers to continuously purchase my products, I had to figure out what makes my business different or unique.

As an entrepreneur, you *want* to be abnormal. This gives your customer a good reason why they should choose you over the rest. Enter **value proposition**, the thing that makes your business different from others.

Finding your value proposition isn't always easy, but is necessary, especially when you are doing something a lot of people are already doing.

Think about it. If a coffee company went on Shark Tank and offered the sharks a sample of their coffee, which tasted like regular coffee, was priced like regular coffee, and had nothing that made it different from other brands, do you think the sharks would invest their money in that business? No! Of course not! That coffee company isn't giving them a reason to buy or invest. It's just the same old coffee you can find in your local grocery store.

The same thing goes for you. If you go onto Shark Tank, and you don't tell them what makes you different from all the other companies out there, the sharks will eat you alive! Make sure that when you create your business, you find what is different about it and what makes it stand out from other brands. This way, your custom customer, avatar, or target market will choose you instead of the competition.

One way of creating a business that has a unique value proposition is by finding out what your customers want, fear, or need. From there, write out how you will not only solve their problem, but also the added benefits of using your product instead of someone else's.

For example, if you are making socks, your value proposition could be that you make socks that keep athletes' feet from getting stinky and sweaty by using odor-absorbing bamboo fibers. Or, they could have a set of unique designs that attract a specific group of sock wearers, like artsy teens.

Take a look at other companies and see what they have to say about the products and services they provide. Have you purchased from any of them? Ask yourself why you chose that one product instead of another. These examples will help you find answers as to what makes you different.

Here is my value proposition statement. It states why I believe my business is different from others out there.

J. BRIELLE HANDMADE GOODS IS A SKINCARE COMPANY FOUNDED BY A TEEN FOR TEENS. WE USE NATURAL INGREDIENTS TO CREATE HANDMADE BATH PRODUCTS THAT MAKE TEEN SKINCARE ROUTINES EASY, SAFE, AFFORDABLE, AND FUN.

You can use this as a template for creating your value proposition by adding to it and replacing the information with things relevant to your business. Creating a value proposition statement is not difficult if you start with the right information, and mindset (remember your first ingredient). You just really need to think about what makes you YOUniquely you and how you should communicate that to your customer.

TIPS FOR YOUR SIXTH INGREDIENT

Tip #1: Never be afraid to be different. If all the flowers in the world were the same, it would be a pretty boring world.

Tip #2: Write out your value proposition and memorize it. Adjust it as often as you need.

Tip #3: Communicate your value proposition to your customer clearly. Give them a reason to choose you!

Complete the *Youniquely You* worksheet by scanning the QR Code found at the back of this book in the resource section.

The Clean Truth About STARTING A BUSINESS for Teens

STEP THREE: MIX AND POUR

MARKETING MIX (THE 4 PS)

BUDGETING BASICS

FINDING FINANCING

The exciting part is mixing all that I have prepared together and seeing the final product. Sometimes it turns out perfect. Other times I have to try again.

GIVE THEM
QUALITY
THAT'S THE BEST KIND OF ADVERTISING

-- Milton Hershey
Entrepreneur, Chocolatier

Seventh Ingredient:
Marketing Mix (The 4 Ps)

I absolutely hate it when I'm playing a game on my phone, or living my best life scrolling through some good memes, and all of a sudden there is an ad. Ugh! They are the worst.

Usually, it's just an advertisement showing someone playing a simple game and failing miserably at it. Or some guy with a Corvette in the background trying to tell me about how he made a million dollars. They are so annoying!

Why then do they even bother to put them up? Well, the thing is a lot of people actually click on those silly ads. Most people want stuff. Stuff to do, stuff to buy, and stuff to use. And although playing a game horribly seems like it wouldn't be the best marketing strategy, it works. Admit it, you've downloaded a few…or ten! No judgment here.

Although all the ads may not interest you, they will interest someone. And that's the goal (remember your custom customer). You see, they aren't looking for everyone to buy, just a percentage of those who see their ad. By doing this, they will reap a ton of sales. This is their ***marketing strategy***.

You must create a marketing strategy too! This is how you will bring your product or service to the attention of your avatar or target market.

Let's first talk about the different places where you can market your service or product. Obviously social media (YouTube, Instagram, TikTok, Facebook, Twitter, etc.) is great for reaching your avatar with advertisements about your product or service.

Creating fun and lively videos using these tools is a simple and inexpensive way to reach a lot of people at one time. Don't know where to start? Take a look at some of the videos you've seen that made you want to buy something. What did the person say or do that got you interested? Write down some ways you can use these videos as inspiration to create your own.

Now, I don't mean copy. I mean get inspired. Always show your unique personality when creating content for social media, even if you're weird like me.

Also, doing interviews with other kidpreneurs, news stations, or local groups can get you in front of potential customers. This may be intimidating at first, but after you do it once it gets easier and easier.

I used to be afraid of speaking in front of people because of how nervous I would get. Now, after speaking to many different groups, doing many interviews, and making videos, I have gotten so much better at it. It still isn't my favorite thing to do, but I am not as nervous as I used to be.

Social media is great for marketing, but there are many other useful ways to get your business out there. For example, tell everyone you know that fits your avatar profile about your product or service. They will in turn tell others. This is called "word of mouth" advertising. Word of mouth advertising is always a go-to. Why? People love to buy things that come with a referral or review.

Think about it. When was the last time you bought something without looking at the reviews? Well, just think of word of mouth as someone giving your product a live review.

Many of my customers refer me to someone else. This is how I get a lot of my business. To do this, you have to have your elevator pitch and a business card ready to go. You may know this already, but since I have your attention, I will tell you anyway.

An elevator pitch is a 20-30 second commercial you give to potential customers about your products or services. Tell your customer what you do, why you do it, and why they need you all while being super persuasive in under half a minute. The more they buy into you, the more sales you will make.

Creating a website is another way to market your business. It gives your customers a place to go online to find all of your products or services. You can google website companies that provide simple templates and hosting for free!

A website is not necessary; however, it does help you get more sales from and information about your customers. This leads me to my next suggestion.

Sending emails is a great way to get in front of your target market. When you are selling at a vendor fair, or if you have a website online, be sure to get email addresses of people buying from you. Even if they don't buy, you should ask for their email address. That way, you can send them reminders about your business later, and they may buy from you in the future.

Finally, supporting a cause or giving back to a charity allows customers to learn more about you and your business. Speaking to kids or volunteering your time to serve others will let them see that you aren't just trying to sell something, but that you have a purpose behind what you do. People are much more willing to buy when they know that there is a good cause involved.

Now that you have an idea of what marketing is, we need to go over the four Ps of marketing in order for your strategy to work. The first P in your marketing strategy is your ***product***. Your product, or service, is what your customer is buying from you. It has to be quality, that is, made to the best of your ability. This is the most important of the four Ps. If you don't have a great product, it will be hard to sell it to your customers.

The next P is ***promotion***. Promotion is how you get customers interested in your product or service. Actually, they are not buying the product, they are buying you.

Not like that. I mean they think that the product is only as good as the person selling it. They have to trust you! So, when you are marketing your product, you really have to put on a show. Whether it's in your pitch at vendor events, or in a TikTok video, you have to make your customers stop and go, "Wow, they know their stuff!"

You've seen other companies use promotion strategies such as issuing a challenge. For instance, in the example I used at the beginning of this chapter, a gaming app may ask, "Think you can do better? Download now to level up and win extra points!" This approach makes some people feel competitive and want to prove themselves, so they download the game to play.

Another promotional strategy is called **exigency**. This technique makes your customer quick to buy because they believe the time they have to purchase is limited. This form of advertising tells them, "Hurry up and buy because time is running out!" Most customers have a fear of losing out on a deal, so this strategy works well.

The third P is **place**. Place is simply trying to get you to think about *where* you are selling. Where have you placed your product or where do you provide your service?

If you plan to get your products in a store or want to sell at vendor events, will your target market be able to reach you there? Do you want to place it in high-end boutiques where only the rich people shop? Are you going to sell only online, or do you want to set up a vendor table at your local farmer's market? You can do both! However, knowing where your target market is likely to find you is important.

If you don't know, be sure to do more research on your custom customer. The more you know about them, the better decisions you can make about where you place your product or service.

The last P is **price**. Don't underprice or overprice your products. Underpricing will make your products seem cheap and thrown together, while overpricing will leave your target market unable to afford them.

One thing I suggest is first finding out how much it costs you to make your product or perform your service. Then add an amount to your cost to give you a **profit margin** when selling to your customers.

Also, look at the prices of your competitors. Does their product have similar ingredients? Does their service match yours pretty closely? Depending on what's all included, lower or raise your price accordingly.

Be sure to ask friends, family, and potential customers that match your avatar what they would pay for your product or service. They will tell you if you are priced too high or too low.

There is another pricing strategy to think about. Have you ever wondered why some products are priced with a .99 at the end instead of just rounded to .00? This has been psychologically proven to attract more customers.

For example, if you were walking down an aisle looking for shampoo and saw a brand you liked for $4.99, and another you like just the same for $5.00, you would most likely reach for the $4.99 bottle. Even though it's only a one-cent jump, your brain makes it seem like a big deal. Even when you read that, the $5.00 was probably less appealing. Consider this tactic when pricing your products as well.

So, to wrap up the seventh ingredient, know that marketing is your way of presenting your business to the world. Understanding how to use the 4 Ps will help you create your marketing strategy.

TIPS FOR YOUR SEVENTH INGREDIENT

Tip #1: Understand the 4ps of marketing and how they can help you create a good marketing strategy.

Tip #2: Always have your elevator pitch ready. This will be Important when opportunities to tell someone about your business arises.

Tip #3: If possible, say yes to Speaking Opportunities. With practice, they will increase your confidence and give your business exposure.

Complete the *4ps of Marketing* worksheet by scanning the QR Code found at the back of this book in the resource section.

IF YOU DON'T KNOW YOUR NUMBERS, YOU DON'T KNOW YOUR BUSINESS

-- Marcus Lemonis
Entrepreneur and Philanthropist

Eighth Ingredient:
BUDGETING BASICS

Budgeting basics for entrepreneurs, or anyone for that matter, is a must. This is a step I didn't take seriously when I first started running my business.

My mom gave me **seed money**. When I ran out and asked for more, she told me I had to figure that part out on my own. How was I supposed to know that I was going to need more supplies before I made more money to buy them? Well, I wasn't keeping track of the money coming into my business through sales, **revenue**, and the money going out of my business to buy supplies, **expenses**.

Without a budget, you are walking aimlessly in a blinding blizzard…stalked by ferocious polar bears of **debt**…with the avalanche of an empty bank account waiting to overtake you. Okay, you get the point.

I can't stress enough how important having a budget is. Even though it sounds like a word used only by your parents or financial advisors, budgeting is something that everyone should know how to do, especially you.

All it means is to simply have a plan for spending your money. Money is a tool you use to acquire things you need or want. You have to use it wisely.

To create a budget, you'll need to follow these simple steps. First, figure out how much money you have to start with. Next, list the most important things you will need to create your product idea or fulfill your service.

Let's use a cupcake business as an example. We will say you are starting with $200 and preparing for your first vendor fair.

Your costs will include materials to make your cupcakes, printing signs for your table, and vendor fees. Because this is your first vendor fair, many of the items you will need, like a table and chair, should come from home. Or, you can borrow them. Remember, keep your expenses as low as possible when first starting:

Investment	Expenses	Revenue	Profits
$200*	Materials $40	$125 cash sales	$90
	Packaging $10	$50 credit card sales	
	Printing $10	$175 total sales	
	Vendor Fee $25		
	$85		

* $200 is your initial investment. Set a portion of this money aside so you can use it for your next vendor fair. It is not included in your profits.

Once you take note of how much money you are starting with and a list of your expenses, be sure to track all of your sales. Then, subtract your expenses from your revenue. Wow, you made $90 in ***profit*** from one vendor fair. Great job!

Keeping your money separated into these categories helps you to track your ***operation costs*** and profits. You can use an Excel spreadsheet, QuickBooks, or Google Sheets to list your expenses, revenue, and other items related to your budget.

Having a budget also lets you know how to use your money. I like to use the 10%, 20%, 30%, 40% rule. That's a lot of percentages! This rule says that ten percent of the money you earn is for giving to your church, a charity, or a cause you support. Twenty percent should go toward savings. Thirty percent for spending, and forty percent back into your business to make more products, or to improve the service you are providing. Of course, you can change these as you need to, but it is a start.

Budgeting is like a road map for your money. And because money is a limited resource you have to use it wisely. At least until you get rich and then you can blow ALL your cash!

Ok, not really. No matter what stage of money-making you are in, a budget is essential. Don't get eaten by the ferocious polar bears of debt!

TIPS FOR YOUR EIGHTH INGREDIENT

Tip #1: Use a budget! If you can budget small amounts of money now, you will be able to manage your money as your business grows.

Tip #2: Money is a tool to build wealth, not wealth itself. Knowing how to use it wisely will help you to run your business effectively and build towards your future.

Tip #3: When budgeting, use the ten, twenty, thirty, forty principle. Adjust the percentages as you need to.

Complete the *Budgeting* worksheet by scanning the QR Code found at the back of this book in the resource section.

THE PLANS OF THE DILIGENT LEAD TO
PROFIT
AS SURELY AS HASTE LEADS TO POVERTY

-- Proverbs 21:5
The Bible

Ninth Ingredient:
FINDING FINANCING

Starting any business requires having some money, whether it is a little or a lot. When I started, I had no money. I asked my mom to help me and she obviously said yes. Now that my business is growing, her willingness to invest more in my big ideas is slowly dying. To continue to grow, I am forced to turn to other financing options. *Hint hint.*

What exactly is ***financing***? Financing is just a fancy term for the money you need to run your business. It allows you to pay for supplies, purchase a website, invest in advertising, and more. And while you may not need money for all of these things just yet, you still need money to get the basic materials to start your business if you don't already have them.

How can you get this money? One of the most common ways to get financing for your business when you are just starting out is by asking your parents, family, or friends to either give you the money or loan it to you.

It will be important to have a good presentation ready on what your idea is, what you need the money for, and ways that it will benefit them or your community. When they see how serious you are about starting your business, they will be more likely to give you money so that you can get started.

Using your allowance, or money you receive from doing other small jobs like mowing lawns, walking dogs, babysitting, doing chores, etc., is another great way to finance your business.

Instead of spending your money on food, clothes, or games, save it until you have enough to make an initial investment into your business. Open a savings account and put your money there so you won't be tempted to spend it in the meantime. This does require you to work outside of your business for a while to earn the cash you need to get started, but only temporarily.

Another way to get money for your business is by seeking out investors. Not necessarily **investors** like the ones you see on Shark Tank. They can be your friends, family, or total strangers that are willing to help you get started. Investors will give you money in exchange for a piece of your business. Still don't understand? Here is an example.

A girl named Ivy wants to start a clothing line. However, she does not have enough money. She only has one hundred dollars. She needs one thousand dollars to get started. What does she do? She goes to nine of her friends and asks them to invest in her business. She tells each of them that they will get 2% ownership of her business if they give her one hundred dollars. They agree and give her one hundred dollars each.

In one year, Ivy's business has earned ten thousand dollars in profits. Since Ivy's friends each have 2% ownership in her company, they will earn 2% of the profits the company has made.

$10,000 x .02 = $200. Ivy's friends have made an extra $100 by investing in her business. Ivy gets 82% of the profits which equals $8200. She can use part of this money to put back into her business. It's a win for everyone. However, investing is a risk. Ivy could have not made any money at all. Then her investors would not have been so happy.

Taking a loan is another way you can finance your business. I would not suggest loans when first starting out, and here is why.

Let's say you use a credit card or ask a bank for $500 and they give you the loan. This is awesome, right? But wait, there is a catch. You have to pay the money back with **_interest_**! Interest is the cost of money. You will have to pay an extra 10% - 20% of the money you borrowed if you don't pay the loan off in a certain amount of time. That could be $50 - $100 more than what you borrowed!

Loans can be a good tool to use at the right time. For now, let's explore better options.

Another way to finance your business is by raising money through **_crowdfunding_**. It's like having a birthday party for your business and everyone brings it money as a gift!

Crowdfunding is when a business gets small amounts of money from a large group of people using an online platform like Kickstarter.

For example, if you are trying to raise $1000 for your business, you can ask your followers and other people on social media to donate $10 or more until your goal of reaching $10,000 is met.

This is great because each person only has to give up a small amount of money. You just have to make sure that you sell your idea well enough that it will make people want to donate.

Participating in pitch contests, applying for grants, and earning money from selling your products or services may all provide financing for your business. No matter how you get it, you will need to use some of the money to put back into your business so that you can continue to grow. Don't spend the money you need for your business on makeup, clothes, food, and other frivolous things. I promise I have never done that!

Using the right mix of financing will help you keep your business growing. Don't worry if you don't have all you need right away. Just keep saving until you do and researching all the ways you can convince other people to give you the money you need. This is what a smart business owner will do.

TIPS FOR YOUR NINTH INGREDIENT

Tip #1: Raise as much money as possible without having to borrow any for as long as you can.

Tip #2: Put money back into your business so that it can continue to grow.

Tip #3: Open a savings account to keep the money you have saved safe until you are ready to invest in your business.

Complete the *Finding Financing* worksheet by scanning the QR Code found at the back of this book in the resource section.

Outro

We have made it through the nine key ingredients I used to turn my soap hobby into a real business. Of course, there are more things we will need to cover in order to continue growing your business, but if you follow these simple steps, you will be off to a great start.

If you remember, at the beginning of the book I told you I wanted to persuade you to become an entrepreneur. Did I convince you?

So, what is an entrepreneur? You are an entrepreneur! Today you are taking the first steps of forging your own path by turning your hobby or passion into a real business. It can be scary, but with God's help, it will be fun, challenging, and empowering.

Teens all across the world have already started. Now it's your turn. You have my nine key ingredients to get you going. All you have to do is get off the couch, dump your secret stash of candy, and get busy.

The world is waiting for you! Are you ready for the challenge? Let's go!

Postface

Hello friend! I hope you enjoyed this book. There will be more tips and tricks to help you grow your business. For now, don't wait. Get started!

Also, come hang out with me on my Facebook page and Instagram @jbriellehmg, or visit my website www.jbriellehmg.com to learn more about what I am doing to support you and other youth entrepreneurs. Ask me questions or send me an email. Remember, we're in this journey together. I can't wait to hear about all of your success!

Your Handmade Friend,
Jordyn

The Clean Truth About STARTING A BUSINESS for Teens

Thank You

Thanks to everyone who helped me write this amazing book so that I can share it with the world. A special thanks to my mother and Mrs. Arriel Bivens-Biggs for guiding me every step of the way and being a continuous source of encouragement. Thank you to my father, brothers, mentors, family, and friends who were all quick to point out a mistake. (Just kidding!) I am so thankful for all of you!

Glossary

Avatar: A fictional character that represents your ideal customer.

Budgeting: A written or recorded plan for how resources, particularly money, will be used.

Crowdfunding: Small amounts of money from a large group of people to fund a business or a project.

Debt: Money that is owed to someone else.

Elevator Pitch: A short and persuasive sales pitch.

Entrepreneur: A person that starts a business and takes on all the risks, but receives the greatest rewards.

Exigency: A sense of urgency or a need to have something right now.

Expenses: The costs a person pays for goods or services.

Financing: A way of providing money a business needs to operate.

Influencer: A person that influences others to buy something or participate in an activity.

Inspiration: Being mentally encouraged to do something creative.

Interest: The cost of borrowing money.

Investor: A person that offers their money or expertise in exchange for earning a profit.

4ps of Marketing: Place, Price, Product, and Promotion.

Marketing Strategy: A plan of action to promote a product or service.

Mindset: A belief or attitude held by a person.

Networking: Interacting with others in order to exchange information and build professional relationships.

Operating Costs: The costs associated with running a business (e.g., materials, website, rent, internet...etc.)

Passion: A strong emotion or desire for something.

Profit Margin: The amount by which revenue exceeds expenses.

Revenue: Money generated from the sale of a product or service.

Seed Money: Money given to start a business or project.

Shorthand: A way of writing that uses symbols or abbreviations when taking notes.

Target Market: A group of customers to whom you are aiming to sell your product or services.

Toxic Positivity: Suppressing true feelings of sadness and frustration in order to appear positive.

Value Proposition: A unique feature of one's business that makes them stand out from the competition.

RESOURCES

Or visit www.jbriellehmg.com/resources

Made in the USA
Columbia, SC
23 October 2021